METROPOLITAN BO

FOX ON THE PAVEMENT

IRENE BYERS

Fox on the Pavement

Illustrated by Gabrielle Stoddart

HODDER AND STOUGHTON
LONDON SYDNEY AUCKLAND TORONTO

*For Donald and Joan who have foxes
living in their garden.*

British Library Cataloguing in Publication Data

Byers, Irene
    Fox on the pavement. – (Brock books)
    I. Title
    823'.914[J]   PZ7

    ISBN 0-340-34757-0

First published 1984
Second impression 1987

Published by Hodder and Stoughton Children's Books,
a division of Hodder and Stoughton Ltd,
Mill Road, Dunton Green, Sevenoaks, Kent TN13 2YJ

Photoset by Rowland Phototypesetting Ltd,
Bury St Edmunds, Suffolk

Printed in Great Britain by T. J. Press (Padstow) Ltd,
Padstow, Cornwall

Contents

Foreword

Many people dislike foxes. Some go as far as to call them vermin to be exterminated whenever possible. With the development of many country areas, foxes have been driven away from their natural habitat and chosen refuge in towns and suburbs. Because he is cunning and clever and has a strong will to survive in these unnatural surroundings, he has won reluctant admiration from many, including myself. For whether we like it or not the fox is here to stay.

My cousins, Donald and Joan, to whom this book is dedicated, have a fox family living in their garden, the earth being driven into their high, boundary hedge. The cubs romp on the lawn with their pet dog, and treat the cats with respect. As in my story, some of the neighbours, together with my cousins, see that they are well fed and cared for. The foxes' presence has caused some inconvenience, but also given many moments of delight.

1
Shock for Paul and Susan

'Time to go, children,' called out Mrs Carter from her folding beach chair. 'It will be nearly nine o'clock before we get home.'

Paul and Susan took a last lingering look at the sun-dappled sea. The day had been a lovely start to their summer holiday outings. For one thing, Dad had managed to get the whole of Saturday off instead of doing two short shifts driving a train, and for another, the weather had been perfect. They had bathed and paddled, stared enviously at the wet suited water skiers, and admired the clever ones who had balanced so securely on a board clinging to the mast of a single sail.

'One day I'm going to have one of those,' said Paul.

'That'll be the day,' said his sister, laughing. 'You already owe Dad two pounds on your new camera.'

'Children, I said "hurry",' their mother began again as she helped her husband to arrange

the large wicker picnic basket, chairs and rugs
into a neat pile. 'If you don't, we shan't have
time for our last treat.'

'I don't think we ought to do more than go
straight home,' said Mr Carter. 'I don't want
to be caught in a traffic jam.'

'No fear of that on the motorway. What's the secret, Mum?' asked Paul, struggling into his shorts and T shirt. 'If it's to be supper at one of the motorway cafés, can I have a giant sized hamburger?'

His mother smiled again. She was short and plump, and had reddish-brown, naturally curly hair in contrast to her children's brown hair, and her face always seemed to be creased in little laughter lines. Susan, who had already dressed, suddenly jumped up and down. 'You and your hamburgers! I can guess where we're going. We're going to eat all our left-overs in Edgeway Wood.'

Paul's face lit up in delight. Like most town children he loved woods, especially Edgeway Wood, and had spent many a happy hour climbing trees and watching the wild animals at play. 'I wonder if I could remember the way to that badger's sett. If we all kept very still we might even see them hunting for food, especially if we get there just before dark.'

With everyone carrying something they piled into their father's car. 'Matty', as they affectionately called her, was very old, but Mr Carter knew almost as much about cars as he did about trains; by saving up and buying spare parts he had managed to keep 'Matty' road-worthy.

At last they were off and heading for the M sign which showed the route to London. Mr Carter had judged the time rightly and there were no hold-ups anywhere.

Susan's gaze darted to the left and right seeing fields of ripening corn, and high banks with clumps of gorse bushes where the motor-way had cut swathes through the countryside. Paul, on the other hand, kept his gaze glued to the right, and suddenly he gave a whoop of delight. 'We're there,' he shouted, 'and in record time. Good old "Matty".'

Mr Carter brought the car to a standstill in a parking place, and with Mrs Carter carrying the picnic basket, they retraced the few yards back. Suddenly all four stopped. Set back among the tall pines was a huge notice board bearing in letters a foot high the words 'DARLINGTON ESTATE. SITE FOR A HUNDRED HOUSES.'

'I don't believe it,' cried Susan, stunned. 'Surely no one would destroy a whole wood. Why, some of these trees must be over a hundred years old.' The four stopped beyond the outer boundaries, and stared aghast. Already the first of the felled trees littered the bracken-brown earth, inches thick with pine needles and cones, their branches and leaves slowly withering.

Paul and Susan ran forward until their way was barred by a Range Rover. Leaning against its side were two men eating thick sandwiches and drinking from two thermos flasks. The younger of the tree fellers glanced round in surprise. 'Hello, you there, where did you spring from? This isn't public property any more, you know. You're trespassing.'

'And you're a wicked man,' shouted Susan, her temper roused. 'You ought to be ashamed of yourself.'

The young man looked amused. 'Hold on, youngster. If my boss decides to buy Edgeway Wood to build houses, and says "clear it", I do just that. I'm only doing the job I'm paid to do.'

'But what about the wild creatures that live here? Where will they go?' said Paul.

'Same as a good many others have to do,' replied the older tree feller with a heartless

11

laugh. 'Find a new patch or go on the dole.'

'Very funny,' said Paul sarcastically. 'You'd think differently if it was happening to you.'

'The kid's got a point. The wild creatures have a right to live same as we have.'

'Don't tell me you're going soft, Dave.'

'Not soft, Fred,' said Dave, 'but sometimes I think there won't be a green spot around here any more. Reckon I saw a young fox this morning. Proper terrified, he looked. Not long left his mother judging by the size of him, and now this happens.' He screwed on the top of his thermos flask and picked up the electric saw. 'One more felling and that will be our quota for the day. Like to see how quickly we saw through this oak, kids?'

Susan looked up at the beautiful stately tree and tears sprang to her eyes. Angrily, she brushed them away. 'I should hate to.'

Paul felt as his sister did and, turning, they ran back to their father and mother.

'I can't bear it,' Susan said to her mother, the tears flowing freely now. 'They're destroying everything in the wood.' She thought of the carpet of bluebells in the Spring, the shiny brown chestnuts they used to gather, the bags

of fir cones that had sweetened the open fire they sometimes lit when the weather was very cold, and all the shady places where they had picnicked. Paul thought again of the trees he had climbed and how once he had surprised a squirrel in its drey. Now day by day the whole wood would be eaten away.

'I know it's hard, Susan,' comforted her mother, 'especially as we love the wood so much, but people need houses too. Maybe there are other woods where the wild animals and birds can go.'

The electric saw stopped whirring and the

tree fell with a sickening crash. Then the wood was quiet. 'Let's just sit here and enjoy our supper.'

'I don't want any,' said Susan.

'And I'm not hungry either,' said Paul. 'I never want to come this way again.'

'Not even to reach the sea?' said his father.

'There are other roads than by the motorway,' said Paul stubbornly. 'You eat your supper if you want to.'

Mr and Mrs Carter looked at each other. They knew how the children felt, but neither could find the words to give comfort. Mr Carter accepted a sandwich, but the first bite threatened to choke him. Edgeway Wood had been part of their lives ever since the children could walk. He, too, felt saddened and, throwing the rest of the sandwich away, he rose to his feet.

'All right. If no one wants to eat, we'd better make for home.'

All four climbed into 'Matty', but the only sound was the splutter of the engine as it nosed its way on to the ribbon of a road that seemed to go on for ever.

2
Rescue

At the same time as the Carter family were beginning their journey home, a fox cub, recently weaned from his mother, was walking along the hard shoulder of the motorway. His whole body rocked with fatigue. Earlier that morning a giant fir tree had crashed, the foliage almost blocking the entrance to his earth. He reeled back to the furthermost corner and crouched there trembling in semi-darkness. After a little while, when he had recovered from his fright, all his instincts urged him to escape. Struggling, clawing with his front paws and pushing with his sharply pointed nose, he at last forced a way through the suffocating density of pine branches. Crouched low, he paused to recover his strength and licked his badly scratched nose and paws. At the same time his alert eyes were fixed on the two figures felling yet another tree. Opportunity to escape came when the tree fellers climbed into the back of the Range

Rover for a short rest. Then, slithering rather than walking and using each patch of scrub as cover, he slowly but surely reached the edge of the wood without being seen.

At noon the sun was high in the sky, but now it was beginning to sink in the West deepening the gold of the corn, and casting long shadows on the high banks of either side of the motorway. In the distance the sodium lamps began to come alight one by one, until they were strung out like a golden necklace.

Being a nocturnal animal, the young cub had at first ducked behind a gorse bush at the sound of approaching cars, but it was soon plain that they were all going too fast to notice him. Gaining confidence he loped along even faster, and at the sight of each tree his spirits rose only to be dashed as he came nearer. There was no copse in which he could find and dig out a new home; nothing but a solitary tree breaking the sky line.

By now his step was not quite so steady and more than once he faltered and lay down to rest for a few minutes. Only dogged perseverance and a growing hunger drove him on.

Half an hour later the first of the sodium

lights shone down on his coat which at this stage was more brown than red, and picked out the white lined, black pointed ears and his thick brush of a tail. Ahead of him stood a small transport café, now shut for the day. The cub approached it cautiously, his greenish-gold eyes and pointed ears alert for the slightest movement. The door of the café remained shut, and there was no sound other than the roar of traffic. Hunger made him bolder, and leaping on to the rim of the litter bin, he thrust his pointed nose in and rummaged amongst the empty tins and discarded paper bags. Luck

was with him. He gobbled up a handful of cold, greasy chips, and two half eaten hamburgers. Then grabbing another promising paper bag he dropped to the ground and began eating both paper and contents. It was then that the accident happened. As he attempted to leap on to the litter bin again, a sharp, jagged sliver of glass embedded itself deeply into the soft underside of his front right paw. The fox cub yelped in pain and licked at the blood that streamed on to the ground. In vain he tried to bite the glass free, but each effort seemed only to drive it more deeply into his flesh and add to his exhaustion.

Holding the injured paw off the ground whenever he could, the cub limped on to the hard shoulder again, leaving a trail of red spots in his wake. At last, too exhausted to go further, he collapsed in a heap at the foot of one of the sodium lit lamp posts. Car after car passed him. One or two of the occupants remarked how careless or wicked it was to abandon a pet dog so near the end of the motorway, but no one stopped to offer aid.

Then 'Matty' came into view. Mr Carter drove in the slow lane and rarely exceeded forty miles an hour, so that Susan and Paul could not fail to notice the animal or the small pool of blood that was gathering about him and staining the white fur of his under belly.

'Oh, how terrible,' cried Susan. 'Somebody has run over a dog.'

'Pull up, Dad. Please, you must,' begged Paul.

'I don't think I dare,' replied his father. 'We're almost off the motorway.'

'But not quite,' continued Paul. ' "Matty" is so small you can park just in front of him. Then we can see how badly he's hurt.'

'I think the children are right,' said their mother. 'I hate these hit–and–run motorists.'

'Oh, very well,' conceded her husband, 'though what you think we can do, beats me. No vet will be on duty at this time of night, even if we knew where one lived.'

Nevertheless 'Matty' was edged on to the hard shoulder and came to a standstill with a grinding of brakes. The two children leapt out and ran back to the stricken animal. The pointed nose rested between the front paws, but at the sight of the children, his lips parted in an ugly snarl and with a sharp, high pitched yelp the fox cub tried to rise to his feet, only to collapse again with pain and exhaustion. Susan and Paul at once noticed the bushy tail and sharply pointed black-edged ears.

'It . . . it isn't a dog, is it? It's a fox cub,' said Susan hesitantly.

Paul nodded. 'I wonder if it's the one the tree feller saw earlier in Edgeway Wood.'

'If so, he's travelled a mighty long way for a youngster. He hasn't even got his red coat yet,' said Mr Carter, joining them. 'No, don't touch him, Susan. He'll most certainly bite you. Fetch my thick pair of leather driving gloves from the cubby hole in the dash-board, Paul, and get your mother to bring the First Aid box. Then I might be able to find out what the damage is.'

Paul ran back and returned a moment later with his mother, the gloves and the First Aid box. Then as her father put on the gloves, Susan bent low and stared into the greenish-gold eyes; ignoring his advice not to touch him, she ran a gentle hand down the cub's head and along his rough coat to the thick brush of a tail. To her surprise he did not struggle, but with an animal's instinct seemed to sense that

he was in kindly hands. Susan repeated the stroking, and at the same time her father lifted first one paw and then the other.

The injury drew a horrified exclamation from all of them. 'Glass! Poor little beast,' said Mr Carter. 'Open the First Aid box, Paul. There might be something we can use in it.'

Paul did as he was asked and lifted the lid. The box revealed a roll of bandage, some plasters, a small bottle of disinfectant and a pair of tweezers.

'Just the very thing,' said his father and, tearing his own big pocket handkerchief into strips he bound the fox's jaws together.

Susan looked upset. 'Did you have to do that, Dad? He'll think of us as enemies.'

'You don't understand, Susan,' answered her father patiently. 'This cub's a wild animal, at the end of his tether, I admit. But I don't fancy a bite from those strong teeth of his.'

Susan did not answer. She knew that her father was right, but all the time he probed with the tweezers, she kept her eyes shut, and continued to stroke and talk lovingly to the cub. Strangely enough, beyond one frantic wriggle and muffled cry, the cub lay still, as if again instinct told him that these humans were trying to ease his pain.

'Got it,' cried Mr Carter at last, holding up the jagged piece of glass. 'Now for the disinfectant. This will sting him a bit, so hold on to him, children, for all you're worth. Then I'll bandage the wound and that will be that.'

Within a few minutes the cub's paw was neatly bandaged, but he made no effort to move even when his jaws were freed. Mr and Mrs Carter laid him gently on the grassy verge, then moved towards the car. Paul and Susan ran after them. 'What do you mean by saying "that will be that"?' asked Paul. 'We can't just leave him here.'

'Of course we can't,' echoed Susan.

'Then what do you suggest that we do? Take him home and offer him a put-you-up in the annexe?'

'I don't find that very funny,' answered Paul, with a flash of temper. 'All I'm saying is that if we leave him now we might just as well have ignored him in the first place. He's miles from his wood now.'

'And I'm trying to say that wild animals belong to the wild. He's a tough one or he

23

wouldn't have got so far, and when he's rested he'll be able to put paw to ground, and in a few days' time he'll begin to gnaw the bandage away. Foxes, even young ones, have a lot of sense.'

Susan's eyes filled with tears. 'He'll starve, I know he will. He's so very little. He needs nursing. Why can't we take him home and keep him until the wound heals?'

'And after that?' queried her mother.

'I don't know,' admitted Paul. 'We'll just have to think of something. I just know that Susan is right.'

Mr Carter ran a hand through his thick brown hair.

'Of course we *could* put him in the shed at the bottom of the garden. All right, children. On your own heads be it. We take him home.'

3
The Watcher

'I shall call him Foxy,' declared Susan.

'Why?' asked her brother. 'I think it's a silly name.'

'No, it isn't. It suits him because he's so small and cuddly, like a toy Grandma gave me when I was little.'

While the children argued, Mrs Carter emptied the remains of the day's picnic then, having lined the large basket with newspaper, she put it back in the boot of the car. Susan and Paul watched silently as their father, still wearing the protective gloves, lifted the injured cub. He fitted perfectly into the make-shift carrier and sniffed hungrily at the meat sandwiches Mrs Carter had tucked into one corner.

'That's the end of your picnic basket,' said her husband. 'However hard you scrub it, you'll never get rid of the smell of fox.' He made as if to close the lid until Paul grabbed his arm. 'You can't shut the lid of the basket or close the boot; he'll suffocate,' he protested.

'Credit me with a little sense,' replied his father with a smile. 'I intend to prop the lid open with two of these large pronged forks and wedge your mother's shortie umbrella under the boot cover. That will give him enough air without the chance to escape.'

'Clever old Dad,' said Susan. 'You think of everything.'

'Matty' seemed to purr as she took to the road again and in spite of a few holdups at junctions, they reached Burley Avenue on the stroke of nine. Number forty-two where the Carter family lived was a neat three-bedroomed house with a narrow side passage separating it from the next block of six houses. A small front garden was gay with marigolds and petunias, and to the rear the main garden, though narrow, was long and cleverly divided between flowers and a small vegetable patch. At the far end against a lowish wooden fence stood the tool shed. Mr Carter had spent three years' savings and more on having an extension built on to the dining room, and this served as a hobby room for the children and a guest bedroom when the need arose.

'Matty' was safely parked at the kerb and

Susan who was first out looked about her. There were no late strollers, but by the light of a full moon she saw the curtain in the downstairs room opposite, move. She knew without being told who the watcher was. Brian Peters was nosy and ever on the watch, so that few activities escaped his inquisitive eye. Susan, although uneasy, decided to ignore the watching eyes and peered through the narrow opening of the boot. The sandwiches had been eaten and Foxy was still asleep. Mrs Carter opened the front door and Paul and her father moved round to the boot. Mr Carter swung it wide.

'Watch it, Dad,' warned Susan. 'That horrid Brian's on the watch again. You'll have to risk closing the basket until Foxy's safely in the shed.'

Mr Carter looked at his children and across to the face now closely pressed to the window-pane. 'Pity that kid hasn't something better to do with his time,' he said at last. 'But why do you and Paul always gang up against Brian? I admit he's nosy, but that's probably because he's an only child and feels left out of things. Why not give him a chance?' As neither of them answered, he gave Paul a powerful torch, and telling him to lock the boot, he removed the two forks, shut the lid firmly and lifted the basket out by the two handles. Foxy, though small, was heavy and Mr Carter stooped a little under the weight; then with the children going on ahead, and guided by the torch he made his way down the twisting garden path and on to the wooden shed furnished with a collapsible work bench and a row of gardening tools. Gently he lowered the basket to the floor in the right-hand corner. Susan lifted the lid, and to her amazement, the fox cub gave her one sleepy look, then shut his eyes again. Covering him with a hessian sack which had once held seed potatoes, she said, 'Poor little thing, he certainly is exhausted. I wonder how he got separated from his mother? I still can't quite believe it. A real live Foxy of our very own.'

Shooting the bolt of the shed, Mr Carter led the way back into the house. It had been a long day and he was tired. 'Don't get too attached to him,' he warned. 'He only stays until he's really fit. I'm not partial to the smell of foxes and they're not as clean as badgers. He's probably covered with fleas already.'

'Pooh! What of it. Cats get fleas too. We can soon do something about that,' said Paul. 'I've got enough pocket money left to buy a tin of anti-flea powder.'

'You're forgetting something,' said his father. 'After a good night's rest, that cub's one instinct will be to escape. He won't see us as friends. We shall be as frightening to him as those tree fellers were, if he did escape from Edgeway Wood. So neither of you must try to handle him unless I or your mum are present. And then only with gloves on. Is that understood?'

'I hate to add another dampener,' broke in Mrs Carter. 'Feeding foxes, even small ones, costs money. Why do you think we're not going away on holiday this summer? Because we haven't finished paying for the extra extension to the house.'

Susan and Paul were silent for a moment. Then Paul said: 'If I took over all the weeding, watering and cutting the grass for you, would that earn me some extra pocket money?'

His father's eyes twinkled, knowing what a hardship gardening was for Paul. 'Quite a bit, Paul. After the long distance journeys and the overtime I have to put in, I haven't much time or energy left for gardening.'

'And we could save all the scraps, and I could hunt for worms and slugs,' said Susan. 'Do you remember how they ate nearly all our lettuces and beans last year. And maybe I could wheedle a meaty bone from the butcher sometimes. I don't think foxes mind what they eat.'

'A pair of schemers, that's what you are,' said their father, as he sat down in his favourite armchair. 'But nothing is altered. He goes when he's better.'

'Where?' asked Paul. 'You can't just dump him even if we do find another wood. I'm told foxes sometimes go for one who doesn't belong there.'

'Not if he found a mate,' said his father.

'Oh, goody! Then that means you *will* keep him until he's old enough to fend for himself.' Susan gave her father a hug.

Mr Carter groaned. 'Oh, bother the pair of you. You make me say things I never meant to. All right. It's a promise. We keep him until he's big and strong enough to fight his own battles.'

Mrs Carter heated milk for mugs of cocoa

and came in carrying a tray laden with plates of sandwiches and biscuits. As she did so the front door bell rang. 'Now who on earth can that be?' she asked. 'I've never known anyone call on us as late as this.'

Paul squinted through a crack in the curtains. 'It's that pest, Brian,' he said in a disgusted tone of voice. 'Let's pretend we've all gone to bed.'

'And left the downstairs lights full on,' replied his father. 'Be your age, Paul. Never make a chap think you're scared of him.'

Paul swung round fiercely. 'I'm not afraid of a squirt like that, and in spite of what you said earlier, I don't think I shall ever like him.'

The bell rang again. Mrs Carter looked helplessly at her family then went to answer. 'Hello, Brian,' she said. 'A bit late in the day to come visiting, isn't it?'

'I suppose it is,' he replied, 'but seeing your lights on, I thought I'd just pop over and ask if you'd all had a good day.'

Mrs Carter ushered him into the sitting room. Two pairs of hostile young eyes looked coldly at him.

'Hello, Paul. Hello, Susan. You had

smashing weather for your trip, Mr Carter. Did you have a picnic in Edgeway Wood on the way home? You usually do.'

'Well, we didn't this time,' burst out Susan impulsively. 'Two horrible men were cutting down all the trees.'

'But according to my Dad, you did.'

'How did he know?' asked Paul.

'Those horrible men as you call them, called in at a pub where my Dad was having a pint and they got talking. You know how it is. One thing led to another and suddenly they mentioned tree felling, and a girl who was upset and how they passed you in the Range Rover. One of them recognised you, Susan, and said you were all bending over something. I was wondering what it was.'

'I can tell you that,' said Mr Carter. 'It was an injured dog. Too small to be away from home. If you want to know the end of the story, which I guess is the reason for your visit, we just bandaged his wounds and took him to a safe place. I'm sorry, lad, but now you'll have to go. It's been a long day and Paul and Susan are tired.' Mr Carter yawned loudly and at last Brian took the hint and left.

'How peculiar. Brian's father meeting the tree fellers, I mean,' said Paul.

'Not so very. Brian's father is a travelling salesman and his area extends well beyond London. Late closing on a Saturday would be a good time to call for him. Thank goodness neither of the tree fellers saw that it was a fox we were helping.'

Susan gave her father another hug. 'Oh, thank you, Dad. What a smashing liar you are.'

'I didn't fib. I believe a male fox is called a dog, just as the female is called a vixen. I may be wrong, of course.'

'Whether you're wrong doesn't matter,' said Paul. 'At least you put Brian off the scent.'

'It's not Brian I'm worrying about. It's quite natural for him to be curious. It's his father. I carried that basket as if it was heavy, and it shouldn't have been after a day's outing. You noticed that Brian didn't mention the torch I gave you, or that the boot of the car was raised. Mr Peters is a bully. He won't even let Brian keep a pet of any sort, and if he worms anything from Brian about our wounded animal, he might become suspicious. And that could spell trouble.'

4
A Bad Day

In spite of their late night, Susan and Paul were up early next morning, and their first thoughts turned to Foxy. They found their mother filling a bowl with bacon rinds, left over scraps of ham and mixed cereal. She also poured milk into a basin. 'Hello, you two,' she greeted them. 'I haven't the faintest idea what foxes eat, but your father won't be a moment or two, so while you're waiting, you can add the luxury of snails and worms if you can find them.'

It had rained overnight, and the worms had cast little mounds of earth on the grass, so that it was not difficult to find them. By careful prodding without disturbing the grass roots too much, Susan soon had half a jar full. 'The birds aren't going to be too pleased,' said Paul, adding his own contribution of snails, 'but with Mum's meal, Foxy's in for a good tuck in.'

Soon, their father appeared and, carrying the

food and drink carefully between them, they watched him slide the bolt back. As they stepped inside the shed, utter chaos met them. The tools were scattered all over the floor, the corner of the work bench was gnawed through, and the sodden lining to the large basket was torn to shreds. Foxy crouched in the left hand corner, snarling and yelping as only an animal in pain can. The bandage on his

paw was ripped to ribbons, and the blood flowed again. None of the food Mrs Carter had left overnight had been eaten, but the bowl of milk was empty.

Mr Carter motioned the children back, and with his hands already protected by gloves, he walked towards the cub. The injured paw was swollen and red, and the cut was oozing a nasty yellow liquid. It was immediately plain that the cub was running a temperature. The children were speechless with dismay. At last Paul spoke. 'Foxy's ill. We'll have to get a vet. He must have gone mad in the night.'

'Delayed shock and the wound probably accounted for it,' replied his father. 'Well, that's the end of our secret, I'm afraid. I'll have to look up the Yellow Pages for the nearest vet; it's a Sunday, but perhaps he'll help. Meantime I'll disinfect the paw, and leave him the food and drink. Then I'll telephone.' Once again the cub's jaws were bound together and once again another bandage took the place of the old. Five minutes later the shed was rebolted.

Mr Carter was as good as his word and as soon as breakfast was over, he looked up the addresses of the nearest veterinary surgeon. He found a Mr Mostyn who lived only ten minutes away. Mr Carter dialled his number and in a rather hesitant and apologetic manner explained the emergency.

'A fox cub, eh,' came the reply. 'You certainly go in for an unusual pet. Well, Sunday or no, we can't let the little beast suffer. I live over the surgery, so call in an hour's time and I'll have something ready for you.'

The children waited impatiently, and once went down the garden and peered through the shed window. Foxy was still huddled in the far corner, his pointed nose between his paws; his eyes glazed with misery and pain. At last the clock showed that the hour was nearly up. Mr Carter checked his petrol supply, and the children waited until the car doors were unlocked. Brian was again watching from the downstairs window. Paul, in an unguarded moment, put out his tongue and received a sharp rebuke from his father. They soon reached Mr Mostyn's surgery, and after a great deal of discussion and a few disapproving remarks from the vet, Mr Carter was handed a box of pills, a jar of anti-biotic cream and some fresh bandages. For good measure the vet also handed

38

over a large sack of sweet smelling straw which he kept for his boarded patients. 'Line the basket each morning and night and disinfect with Dettol,' he said, 'otherwise the shed will reek of fox.' Paul put his hand in his pocket. 'And I want a tin of anti-flea powder,' he said.

'Good idea.' Mr Mostyn took one down from a shelf. 'Dust him all over with this, then in two days' time, comb and brush him thoroughly. But of course if he doesn't improve by then, you'll have to bring him down to me for further examination. I've had some odd pets to deal with, but never a fox.'

The family thanked the vet for his willingness to help, especially as it was a Sunday, but Mr Mostyn merely shrugged his shoulders. 'Like doctors, we have to be ready for all sorts of emergencies. But when the cub does get better, you'll have the problem of exercising him. Foxes are used to roaming.' So saying, he took a slim dog's collar and lead from a hook and gave it to Paul, and waved his hand as Paul protested. 'No money. I think you're a crazy family, but the collar and lead belonged to a sick animal that didn't make it. So it's yours from now on. Train him gradually; take him for walks at dusk and see how he reacts.'

The children were loud in their thanks; Mr Carter paid for his purchases and the fee and in no time 'Matty' was once more outside their home. Brian was kicking a football outside his house and looking at a loose end. He watched the unloading of the sack with especial interest.

'What's in that?' he asked Susan. 'You keeping rabbits all of a sudden.'

Susan thought quickly. 'No, it's straw to protect our strawberry plants from slugs.'

'All that straw for six strawberry plants,' scoffed Brian. 'You must be kidding. You brought that wounded dog home with you. I know you did. Your father's fib didn't fool me. But why make a mystery of it?'

'We're not. We didn't bring a wounded dog home with us, but even if we did, it's none of your business, so buzz off,' said Paul. He slammed the front door.

'No need for that, Paul,' said his father. 'I thought I told you to lay off Brian.'

'Sorry, Dad. But he does something to me.'

'And me,' echoed Susan. 'I don't know why, but I'm suddenly scared.'

'Then you're being very silly,' said her

father. 'I'm worried for quite another reason. I'm on the Edinburgh run tomorrow and shall be away overnight. I can't change the rota, so you and your mother will have to manage as best you can. So lesson one starts now. I shall need both of you to help me get the pill down. Paul'll hold on to the upper jaw and Susan the lower, so put on your thickest gloves.'

Protected in this way and armed with the pills, the ointment and the sack of straw, they hurried down to the shed. The cub eyed them balefully, but there was little fight left in him. Susan cleared out the evidence of the night's battle, then disinfected the basket and lined it thickly with straw. Then with her father holding the tablet, she and Paul forced open the cub's jaw. Deftly, Mr Carter pushed in the pill, and clamping the jaws tight, pinched the cub's nose. A second later he was forced to swallow it. Bandaging the paw was not so easy. Summoning his last strength the cub limped round and round the shed, yowling pitifully.

'Oh, gosh, Dad, stop him,' cried Paul. 'Everyone in the nearby houses will hear him. And no dog ever made a noise like that.'

His father acted swiftly. Cornering the

protesting cub he bound up his jaws and put him in his basket. The ointment was cool and soothing, and Foxy suddenly became quiet and unresisting. With his jaws free again, he even ate a morsel or two from the plate Susan held out, and drank from the bowl of milk. The golden-green eyes blinked once or twice, then shut. Safe in his cosily lined bed, Foxy slept.

Leaving the rest of the food and drink beside him, Mr Carter put the tablets, the ointment and the bandages on a high shelf, then having straightened his tools and propped the sack of straw against the work bench, he tip-toed after the children. After bolting the door, he looked down at them from his six feet and smiled. 'A small victory, I think, and hardly won.'

'Wait till tomorrow,' said Paul. 'If he's eaten and drunk, we shall know he's over the worst.'

5
The Secret is Out

Next day the improvement was noticeable. Not only was the dish of food and the milk bowl empty, but the bandage was undisturbed and the bright, alert look had returned to the cub's eyes. He was even able to put his paw to the ground without discomfort and he took a step towards the children eyeing them cautiously. Susan held out a gloved hand and to her great joy he accepted the tit-bit she offered. Then he drank from the bowl of milk Paul held out.

Mrs Carter, who had just seen her husband off on his long journey, was also delighted, but still a little apprehensive. 'We've still got to get the pill down and renew the bandage,' she said.

'Leave it to us, Mum,' said Susan. 'Dad showed us how to do it.' But Foxy solved the problem for her. As Susan took out one of the pills, he suddenly gave a huge yawn, and deftly she threw the pill into his open mouth. With a surprised gasp the cub swallowed it. Then it seemed as if another miracle happened. Foxy held out his injured paw and placed it on Paul's knee. Paul, gloves on hand, unwound the soiled bandage and renewed the dressing, then dusted him liberally with anti-flea powder. Susan stroked the cub's head and murmured quietly to him meanwhile. Paul was so pleased that he wanted to try the collar and lead, but his mother was firm. 'No, Paul. It's early days yet. We'll leave the shed door open and if he wants to hobble about the garden, he can. The back door is bolted and the fences are sound, so if you want to, you can watch from the annexe window.' Paul and Susan agreed to this plan and leaving the food and drink with Foxy safely back in his basket, they returned to the house. Promising them another outing on their father's next rest day, Mrs Carter gave them both jobs to do, but every so often they peered out of the back window. The garden remained empty throughout the day hours. Paul mowed the grass. Susan weeded and hunted for slugs and snails. Afterwards both of them went with their mother to the local shops. While at the butcher's they had the misfortune to run into Brian's mother. Mrs

Peters was tall and thin with straight hair shoulder length and dresses that made her look a teenager. Susan and Paul disliked her almost as much as they did Brian.

'Why, hello, Mrs Carter,' she began affably enough but at the same time noticing the request for a marrow bone with some meat left on it. 'Brian tells me you rescued a wounded dog on the motorway last Saturday. Bit of an expense for you seeing that you aren't able to go away this year, isn't it? Dogs cost a lot to feed and there's the licence as well.'

'She's almost as nosy as Brian,' thought Susan.

Her mother's cheeks flushed. 'I think Brian jumped to a lot of wrong conclusions,' she said at last. 'My family like soup and there's nothing better than a marrow bone.'

'Then I'm sorry,' said Brian's mother. 'No offence meant. It's just that my son's got a way of putting two and two together, and what with the sack your children carried on Sunday morning, and the packages your husband was holding, he was sure he was right.' She sniffed loudly. 'And if he is, I don't see why you have to be so secretive about a good turn like that.'

Mrs Carter smiled and after a polite good-bye, she accepted her parcel and left the shop. 'Oh dear, everything is getting so involved,' she said. 'Brian's mother is an awful gossip.'

'But you didn't give anything away, that's the great thing,' said Paul.

Back at the house Mrs Carter put the kettle on for tea, and the children looked out of the annexe window. The sun had dropped behind the houses and Foxy was rolling on his back on the lawn, waving his four paws in the air. Holes in the flower beds showed where he had been digging. There was earth on his pointed nose and uninjured paw. Three marigolds in

47

full bloom lay on their sides. Paul and Susan rushed out into the garden, then stopped short. Having climbed on to their dustbin, Brian was now peering over the door leading to the garden. His face was one big grin.

'Some dog!' he scoffed. 'That's a fox cub. Nothing but a dirty lump of vermin. My Dad says they ought to be exterminated like rats.'

Paul's face reddened with anger. 'Say that once again and I'll belt you one.'

Brian repeated the taunt. Susan acted promptly. Shooting back the well oiled bolt, she lifted the latch and swung open the door. Taken by surprise, and off balance, Brian fell forward on to the Carters' narrow stone patio. Paul gave him a chance to regain his feet, then went for him with doubled up fists. The first blow landed on Brian's nose causing it to bleed. Brian reeled back, then set about Paul. Paul rocked from a right hand blow, to his shoulder. 'You're not much better than vermin yourself,' he shouted. Brian aimed another which caught Paul below the belt causing him to double up with pain. Infuriated, Susan kicked again and again at Brian's shins until he, too, cried out in pain.

48

'Take that and that,' she cried. 'You're not only a creep. You're a real nasty.'

Attracted by the noise and the scuffling, Mrs Carter opened the kitchen door. Brian was pulling Susan's hair, and trying to dodge her repeated kicks. Blood still streamed from his damaged nose, and Paul was still doubled up and trying to regain his breath.

'Whatever's going on between you three? Stop it at once, Brian, and that goes for you, too, Susan. You ought to be ashamed of yourselves. Now come on, own up. Who started it?'

'Brian was using our dustbin lid to do his snooping,' said Susan. 'He saw Foxy and called him vermin. So then I unlocked the door and he fell forward, and then Paul hit him. Serves Brian jolly well right. And he doesn't even fight fair. He hit Paul below the belt.'

'That's enough, Susan. I don't want to hear another word. You were all in the wrong; Brian for trespassing down our sideway and Paul for starting the fight. You're old enough to know that fights solve nothing.'

Brian scowled at the ground. 'I know I shouldn't have snooped, but it's you who will be sorry one day. Fox cubs grow quickly and they gobble up everything small on four legs.'

'You couldn't be more wrong,' said Paul. 'Foxes don't go for domestic pets.' As he said this a ginger cat strolled across the small lawn, stared curiously at the still rolling about cub, then having licked his ear, walked unconcernedly away.

'You see,' said Susan.

'Wait till he's older. He'll spell trouble for all of you.'

'We'll face that when the time comes, Brian,' said Mrs Carter. 'Now inside all of you, and let me see what I can do to wash away some of the battle scars.' She swabbed Brian's swollen, bleeding nose with cotton wool.

'Can't do much about your shins, Brian. You're going to have some lovely coloured bruises in a day or two.' Then she gave Paul a dose of anti-nausea medicine to ease the effect of Brian's hit below the belt, and combed Susan's hair into some sort of order. Standing back she surveyed her handiwork. 'At least you look more like human beings.'

Suddenly the beginnings of a smile lingered about Brian's mouth. Paul gave a half smile in

51

return. 'No more snooping down the side way, Brian?'

Brian shook his head. 'But I can't promise to keep your secret. You don't know Dad when he gets a bee in his bonnet. He'll keep on and on at me until he gets at the truth. I'm sorry. I'll hold out as long as I can.'

'It won't matter. We aren't breaking the law,' said Paul. 'He can't do anything.'

'No, that's true. He can't. But I hope you won't hold it against me.'

'Not if you use the front door when next you come.'

It was a beginning and Mrs Carter ought to have been pleased, but she was still uneasy. 'Oh dear, I hope there won't be any trouble from his parents,' she said when Brian had gone. 'But knowing Mr Peters I feel there might be.' She glanced towards the garden. 'Just look at the state of the flower beds. Holes everywhere and some of my best marigolds uprooted. Foxy certainly can't be allowed to run loose. You'll have to try the collar and lead, Paul.'

'I'll go and get it now,' he answered. Susan dangled the collar in front of Foxy's nose, and when she slipped it over his head, the struggle was short-lived. Soon, brushed free of the flea powder and harnessed to the lead, he was led round and round the garden and allowed to forage for snails and slugs among the vegetables. Mrs Carter replanted her marigolds in the faint hope that they would revive then filled in the holes.

When Susan joined her mother some ten minutes later, she found her unusually quiet. 'Foxy's really a gardener's friend,' she began, eyeing her mother anxiously. 'He's almost rid Dad's vegetable plot of slugs and things. Is something worrying you, Mum?'

'Yes. You don't know how I hated to see you three fighting, and if Mr and Mrs Peters pick a quarrel things will be even worse.'

'I don't think that will happen,' said Susan comfortingly. 'If Brian really wants to be friends, he'll own up that he was trespassing. And it isn't the first time he's gone home looking the worse for wear. He's not very popular at school either.'

'Poor Brian. I almost feel sorry for him. If only your father could have been home. Perhaps none of this would have happened.'

6
Foxy Disappears

The following days saw a rapid improvement in Foxy's condition. A reddish tint crept into his fur and he began to look less like a cub. By now he was completely at ease with the Carter family and even spent part of the day sleeping on a mat in the sunny annexe. As they feared, Brian gave way under his father's persistent questioning and the news about Foxy spread rapidly. The door bell rang frequently. Not all callers were friendly, but the majority were. They saved their scraps and some even brought tins of dog's meat and cartons of milk.

'Reckon you've got a sort of unpaid gardener,' said one neighbour, jovially. 'Wouldn't care to lend him to me for a day or two? Snails are a proper menace this year.' He produced a bag full of large specimens. Mrs Carter shuddered a little as she took it from him, but accepted all the gifts gratefully.

She was especially grateful to Mr Patel, an Indian who ran a local grocery shop and was an excellent carpenter. He called one day accompanied by his daughter, Gita. Gita was a shy girl with the biggest brown eyes Susan had ever seen. Mrs Carter took both her and her father to visit Foxy whose back legs were dangling over the edge of the basket.

'If I might say so,' said Mr Patel, 'your Foxy has outgrown his basket and needs a larger sleeping place.'

'Dad could fit you up with something,' said Gita.

Mr Patel nodded and within three days he produced a deep rectangular box with a removable metal tray lining to the bottom. All the Carter family were delighted. The tray could be slid out each morning, washed and disinfected.

'A clean cub is a healthy cub,' said Mr Patel. 'He'll now have room to curl about as he wishes.'

Gita looked at Susan and smiled. 'My mother would love you all to come to dinner next Friday.'

Mr Carter regretted that he would be on duty, but the rest of the family accepted with alacrity.

'I wonder what they will give us to eat,' said Paul. 'I hope it won't be too spicy.' On the day their slight doubts were soon put to rest. Mrs Patel, wearing a lovely sari with gold edging, produced a mild curried chicken. She, like Mrs Carter, was short and plump and cheerful. Paul looked at the side dishes holding nuts, coconut, sliced banana and chutney. Seeing him hesitate, Mr Patel, who only had an hour's break from the shop, handed him a

spoon and invited him to take a little from each. Mrs Patel handed round a dish piled high with poppadums, wafer thin biscuits cooked on a griddle. 'If you do not like everything just leave it,' she said. 'We shall not be offended.' Paul did like everything and so did Susan and her mother. Soon their plates were empty, and no one except Paul and Mr Patel had appetite left for the semolina sweet dish.

Mr Patel went back to his shop. Susan and Gita did the washing up, leaving Paul and his mother to look at a collection of Indian prints that Mrs Patel showed them. Mrs Carter remarked how different life must be for them in England. Mrs Patel smiled. 'We were sad at first. We did not like our first house, but now we have moved into this road we are happy. The shop thrives and you and others like you have made us feel welcome. Only one or two, how do you say it, give us the cold shoulder. It is a funny term. I hope Gita and Susan will be good friends. It is lonely being an only child.'

As she said this, Gita and Susan burst into the sitting room as if they had been friends for life, and Susan told her mother of the lovely colourful saris that hung in Gita's cupboard.

'But they are for special days only,' said Mrs Patel. 'Gita much prefers jeans and T shirts. Next term when she joins you at your school, Susan, she will dress as all the other girls dress. A blouse and skirt are so sensible.'

'But so dull,' said Susan. 'Don't worry about the first few days, Gita. Everyone feels strange. I'll look after you and show you the ropes.'

The talk went on, and suddenly Mrs Carter looked at her watch. 'Good gracious! It's nearly half past four and your father will want his tea and Foxy his supper.' Telling Gita that she could call whenever she wanted to, the Carter family repeated their thanks and hurried home.

'Aren't they kind and nice,' said Susan. 'I think Gita is beautiful, don't you?'

Foxy was fed and at dusk taken for a short walk round the streets and the nearby common. Sometimes Brian joined them and scoffed at Paul's nervousness. 'What are you worrying about? No one's given him so much as a glance. To them Foxy looks like a young Alsatian puppy.'

At the end of a fortnight, Foxy was free from

fleas and bandages and even tolerated Gita's handling. Every morning the removable base was cleaned, disinfected and covered with fresh straw. The soiled straw was burned. Mr Patel renewed their stock from some of his packing cases and Brian contributed scraps from his mother's dustbin. It seemed as if the whole road had adopted Foxy.

Then without warning, he disappeared. When Paul and Susan went down to give him his breakfast, the door was bolted, but the shed was empty. Both children looked at each other in disbelief. 'How did he escape?' asked Susan at last.

Paul pointed to the left hand wall of the shed. Six slats of wood had been gnawed through leaving enough space for the fox cub to squeeze through.

'There's your answer,' he replied. Paul stared at the pieces in a puzzled manner, then gathered them up and carried them into the kitchen.

'Foxy's escaped,' burst out Susan. 'He must have gone in the night.' She burst into tears and refused to be comforted. Paul held out one or two pieces of wood. 'Do you see anything odd about them, Dad?' he asked.

'I don't see any teeth marks, if that's what you mean. To my way of thinking these slats have been sawn through in an up and down manner. Someone deliberately helped Foxy to freedom.'

'That's what I think,' agreed Paul.

'But the side door is still bolted,' said Susan. 'If he did gnaw the wood through, could he have jumped that?'

Her father nodded. 'It's quite possible. It's also possible that someone let him out, stood on the dustbin and used a long stout stick to shoot the bolt back into position. I always keep the lock well oiled.'

Susan and Paul looked at each other. One thought and one thought only was in their mind. 'Brian,' they both said together.

'Now steady on, both of you,' warned their father. 'That's not fair. Brian's proved himself a friend, and I thought you'd both forgotten and forgiven that scrap you had some time back. You've no proof, so you can't accuse anyone. Several other people in the road disliked the thought of a fox, remember. I'm sorry, my dears, but maybe it's for the best.

Foxy was growing very fast, and freedom is sweet to any wild animal.' He glanced at his watch. 'Now what about a run out somewhere in "Matty"?'

'Only if you tour the neighbourhood and look for Foxy.' A sudden doubt struck Paul. 'Surely if someone used a saw, we should have heard it?'

'No,' replied his father. 'Our bedroom is at the front, and you two sleep even through a thunderstorm. All right, if you insist. We three will make up a search party, but remember Foxy's got a few hours start on us.'

'First I'm calling on Brian,' said Paul stubbornly. 'One look at his face and I shall know.'

In spite of his father and mother's protests, Paul was determined and, with Susan accompanying him, he knocked at the house opposite. Mr Peters opened the door. He was a short, thick-set man, with a balding head and a hint of a moustache on his upper lip. His greeting was unfriendly.

'What do you two kids want?' he asked. 'A bit late in the day to come over and say you're sorry. Two against one isn't my idea of a fair fight. If it hadn't been for Brian, I'd have been over to sort things out with your Dad. And all over a filthy animal like a fox. Don't let me set eyes on him, that's all.'

Paul bit back the news of Foxy's disappearance and squeezed Susan's hand in warning. 'We think it was silly to fight too. And Brian and I are friends now. We've come over to ask if he'd like to come for a short run in our car. It's Dad's rest day.'

Brian's father appeared slightly more friendly. 'Now that's a move in the right direction,' he began, 'but I'm afraid you've chosen a bad day. Brian's been in bed since tea time yesterday with a bad tummy upset. Touch of summer flu, I think.'

'Oh, I am sorry,' said Paul, backing towards the front gate. 'I hope he'll soon be better.'

'I'll tell him you called. He'll be all right tomorrow.'

As the front door shut, Susan looked at her brother. 'Do you believe him?'

'Brian's too fond of his tummy to feign a bilious attack. That lets him out all right.'

Disconsolately they went down the narrow side passage to their own garden. Mrs Carter stood on the kitchen step. 'Well, where did that bit of detective work get you?'

'Right back to Brian's bedroom,' answered Paul. 'According to his father he's been down and out with a bilious attack since yesterday tea time. Where's Dad?'

'Messing about with a bag of Plaster of Paris down by the shed.' Susan and Paul found their father kneeling by the damaged side of the shed.

'What's up, Dad?' asked Paul.

His father glanced up. 'Remember the story of Cinderella and the shoe she left behind. Well, I haven't exactly found a shoe, but amongst Foxy's footprints, I've found the imprint of two human shoes. It rained during the night, so I've been able to take a cast of the best one, and when it sets we'll have our first clue. While we wait for the plaster to dry, we'll drive "Matty" slowly round the neighbourhood. Keep your eyes open for disturbed dustbins, and anything that moves on roofs and garages. Foxes are nocturnal animals in their natural state, so now it's likely that Foxy will hide somewhere and sleep during the daytime.'

An hour's slow driving brought no results. A few empty bags littered a sideway, a couple of cats sunned themselves on garage roofs, but of Foxy there was no sign.

During the ride Paul told his father of Brian's sickness and disheartened they returned to number forty two and immediately thought of the cast their father had taken. The plaster had set firmly. With infinite care Mr Carter freed it from the imprint and turned it sole side uppermost. There plain for all to see were marks indicating a rubber soled shoe.

'A left-footed one at that,' said their father. 'Find the owner of a pair of shoes this size and pattern and you have the culprit. Size eight is my guess.'

'Brian has big feet,' said Paul, all his former suspicions reviving. ' "Shoveller" they call him at school.'

'But Brian has a cast iron alibi,' reminded his father.

7

Noises in the Night

Next day the search continued, but before they could set out, Brian called. He arrived soon after breakfast and looked eagerly at Susan and Paul. 'I wondered if there was any chance of a ride in "Matty". I'm feeling much better.'

'Not today,' said Paul. 'I'm sorry. Dad's working until tea time. Besides we've got other things to do.'

'What other things?' Brian looked searchingly at them. 'Something's happened, hasn't it? You two look just about as glum as an underdone banger.'

'If you must know, we've lost Foxy,' blurted out Susan. 'It's what you always thought would happen, isn't it?'

'Why do you sound so unfriendly all at once?' Brian looked genuinely upset. 'I know I once said a lot of things about that cub, and nothing will ever make me really like foxes. But I know how much Foxy meant to you. I can still remember that blow you dished out, Paul.' He touched his nose. 'Dad wanted to come over and pick a row, but I said I started the whole thing. I'm sorry I let the cat out of the bag, but once Dad starts digging in, he wears a chap down. How did he escape?'

Paul looked at his sister. 'Come and see.' Brian followed them down to the damaged side of the shed and fingered the many pieces of wood that had once been slats. He looked puzzled. 'Very odd. These jagged edges weren't made by teeth, even though the wood is worn enough for a fox to gnaw through.'

'That's what we think,' said Paul, grimly. 'Someone made escape easy for him. But you wouldn't know anything about that, would you, because you were sick?'

Brian looked up at the doubting face. 'You don't believe me. You . . . you think I'd do a rotten thing like that?'

'You could have faked a bilious attack,' said Paul.

A dull red stained Brian's cheeks. 'All right. If that's what you think, think it. You can jolly well go to the Police Station without me.'

'What are you talking about?' Paul looked bewildered at the sudden turn of the conversation.

'Simply that an uncle of mine is a desk sergeant at the local Police Station, and it suddenly struck me that he might know if a fox had been sighted or picked up during the night. He might even have been on a night patrol himself.' Brian slouched away, his head hanging.

'Hey! Wait a minute. I'm sorry. I admit we did suspect you, but now I know I was wrong. If you'll take us, we'll come.'

'On one condition. Susan stays out of it. Girls are a nuisance.'

Susan bit her lips. 'Brian Peters, who do you think you are? You may have a cast iron alibi, but that's no reason for throwing your weight about. Where Paul goes, I go.'

Brian shrugged his shoulders and gave in, but was even less pleased when they met Gita at the front gate.

'I've brought some scraps for Foxy,' she said. Susan told her the sad tale and that now they were going to the Police Station.

'Can I come too?' Gita asked. 'The Police Sergeant is such a kind man. He rescued my cat from a high branch of our tree.'

'Girls!' exclaimed Brian again. 'Like Foxy,

Gita should have stayed in her own part of the world.'

Susan rounded on him. 'Brian, you're slipping again. I warn you. One more word out of you and you can stay in *your* own small corner from this moment onwards.'

Brian lapsed into silence. At the local Police Station the desk sergeant nodded to his nephew and listened to Paul's story. 'Brian wondered if you had picked him up on the night patrol.' The sergeant's eyebrows shot up in astonishment. 'A fox cub in this vicinity. If you didn't act and sound so serious, I'd say you were joking. I know they've got lots of foxes in other suburbs of London, but in all my years of duty, I've never seen hide or hair of one hereabouts. More or less tamed him, had you? Then all I can say is that some folk have strange tastes in pets. Still, I'll tell the squad to keep a look out, and get you to write your name and address here.' He pushed a book forward and Paul did as he was asked, adding LOST. ONE FOX CUB. ANSWERS TO THE NAME OF FOXY. 'If we do come across him,' the sergeant went on, 'it'll be more a case for the R.S.P.C.A., I reckon.'

'Not Paul's Foxy,' said Gita. 'He and his sister were only keeping him until they could find a safe and natural place for him to live in.'

'I see. Just a minute. I've suddenly had a thought. Have you searched the Common?'

'There isn't any shelter there,' said Susan. 'Nothing but open grassland.'

'I know. But what about the copse a quarter

of an hour's walk from there? It used to be part of the grounds marking the boundary of the Old White House. Now the Council has turned it into a home for old people and the copse has become part of the Common. Plenty of tree shelter there. And while I'm about it, take one or two of these programmes. Ought to appeal to you children – side shows and races and all proceeds in aid of the very people I've been talking about.' Paul took a couple and with the encouraging information fresh in his mind, he led the way out of the Police Station.

The copse was not hard to find, but although they spread out in different directions and shouted Foxy's name at the top of their voices, no fox cub appeared.

At last they went home. Paul was disappointed, but at the same time he had a curious feeling that Foxy was somewhere near. He said nothing, however, and glanced down at the programme. 'Hoopla, roundabouts, stalls and races for grown ups as well as young,' he read out.

'That should suit my dad,' boasted Brian. 'He's a smashing jogger. I bet he could beat your dad by a mile. Driving a train all day can't make him much of an athlete.'

'Nor can sitting in a car and calling at stores and peddling things,' retorted Paul.

Both boys scowled at each other. Susan and Gita stepped between them. 'At it again, Brian,' said Paul's sister. 'You ask for trouble every time you open that big mouth of yours.'

'I'm sorry. I always seem to say and do the wrong thing. But my dad is a good racer,' Brian persisted. 'He gets up every morning before light winter and summer and goes for a two mile jog. I know, because I hear his alarm clock go off.'

'Nobody's contradicting you,' said Susan, 'but you can save your boasting until the day of the fête. Let's hope it's one of Dad's rest days.'

Gita accepted Mrs Carter's invitation to lunch, but she left soon afterwards saying she was going to make some paper flower garlands. 'My mother has already been put in charge of the Indian stall.'

'If only we had Foxy everything would be perfect,' said Paul. 'We could charge ten p. for people to see how we handle him.'

'What a perfectly horrible idea,' protested

Susan. 'Foxy's not a freak to be gawped at. I just want to know he's safe.'

That night all the Carter family were tired, too tired even to watch their favourite television programme. 'Something about today's run was worse than all the others,' said Mr Carter. 'Maybe I couldn't get Foxy out of my mind.'

'Neither could we,' said Paul. 'Even Brian seemed to be upset.'

'Why shouldn't he be?' said his father listening to an account of the day's happenings. 'That was a good idea of his to go to the Police Station. Now off to bed all of you, or I'll have to borrow a couple of matchsticks to keep my eyes open.'

Susan and Paul slept heavily for the first part of the night then a sharp clattering of a dustbin lid on the pavement roused both of them. Sister and brother met on the landing each with a pullover pulled over their night clothes and slippers on their feet.

'Cats?' queried Susan.

'Wind!' whispered Paul.

'Foxy,' they both said together, and hurriedly crept downstairs. Paul took down the collar and lead, unbolted the kitchen door and eased open the side entrance. Together they crouched and waited. Another dustbin lid fell and clattered on to the road. This time it was nearer.

'Be careful not to scare him,' warned Paul, his every muscle tense with expectation. The wait was long and unrewarding. An hour later when the stars were paling in the sky, and their hands were stiff with the chilliness that precedes dawn there was no patter of paws down the side way.

'We ought to have gone after him,' said Paul. 'We've mucked our chance. He's slipped away again.'

'Never mind,' said Susan. 'There will be other nights. We'll explore the copse a bit more thoroughly tomorrow; perhaps take a picnic supper and invite Gita and Brian.'

'Good idea,' said her brother. 'Four of us on the watch ought to bring results.'

Tomorrow, however, dawned cloudy and wet, so although the invitations were accepted by Brian and Gita the picnic had to be postponed. But on the Thursday the sun was again shining, and Mrs Carter although inwardly wondering why it had to be a picnic supper, asked no questions. She packed hamburgers, sausages and rolls and added bags of salted crisps. With a tin of Coca-Cola each, the newly purchased, smaller picnic basket was filled.

'Where are we going to eat?' asked Brian as Paul walked purposefully towards the copse bordering the Old White House. 'I'm starving.'

'You'll see in a moment,' replied Paul coming finally to a halt on the fringe of an enormous weeping willow. 'This gives us a splendid look-out spot in case Foxy's out on the hunt. It's a good job there's a children's paddling pool quite near or I don't know how he'd manage to drink. Now let's eat and watch.'

Susan spread out the good things on a small blue and white checked table-cloth, and Brian snapped open a tin of Coca-Cola. As he began drinking he almost choked. 'Paul,' he managed to whisper. 'I may be wrong but I think I saw Foxy's brush disappear round that bush.' He pointed to the right.

'Action,' said Paul. 'We'll each take a different direction and try to corner him. But on no account scare him. If you do get near him give a loud whistle.'

'I can't whistle,' said Gita, 'but Foxy knows me, so I'll just clap my hands.' The four set off in pursuit, getting more and more tired and puffed as they pushed their way through rough undergrowth and peered round and under bushes. Suddenly Brian whistled, but when the others joined him, the animal crouched underneath a gorse bush turned out to be a young Alsatian. His worried owner came running up with collar and lead and thanked them for cornering him. 'He gave me the slip, the young rascal, but how did you know where to look for him?'

'We didn't,' said Paul. 'We were looking for someone else and only came on him by chance.'

'Thanks all the same,' said the man, giving his dog an affectionate pat. 'It's the lead for you, old chap, for the next few weeks. Perhaps that will teach you to obey my call.'

Susan looked at her brother. 'I'm tired and I'm fed up.'

'Me, too,' said Gita.

'It was all my fault,' said Brian. 'I ought to

have seen that it was a dog. But don't let's waste the picnic. Perhaps we'll have more luck if we come another time.'

They returned to their chosen spot and looked down at the cloth in amazement. Not a hamburger, sausage, roll, or salted crisp re-mained. Even the tins of Coca-Cola had been rolled half way down the slope. Paul had to laugh. 'Foxy by name and Foxy by nature. You have to hand it to him. He's certainly pulled a fast one on us this time.'

8
The Mystery is Solved

During the next few nights, Paul and Susan again heard the noise of dustbin lids falling, but although they were quick to follow, and once saw Foxy scattering the contents with his paws, they were never stealthy enough to catch him unawares. Intent though he was in his search for food, he was always quick to sense when human beings were about. Then like a hare he bounded up the hill, and turned the corner leading to the Common. Both knew that it was useless to continue the chase.

It was then that Paul made his plan. He told no one about it except his sister. 'I shall take my sleeping bag and keep watch somewhere where we tried to have our picnic. I shall make it Wednesday because Thursday is Dad's long shift, and he always goes to bed early the night before.'

'I don't like it,' said Susan.

'Don't worry. I won't stay out longer than midnight. You must see that the side door is unlocked, and if you're asleep when I get back, I'll throw some gravel up to your bedroom window, then you can creep down and let me in. I know it sounds mad, but I've got a real hunch that our picnic spot was plumb in the middle of his route to the paddling pond.'

'I still don't like the idea,' said Susan. 'Neither would Mum or Dad. They'd be hopping mad. Supposing you were caught and had up for what do they call it . . . vagrancy.'

'Silly, I shall tell them the truth. You've got to help me, Susan. Without you I'm sunk.'

Wednesday evening came at last, and as he had said, both Mr and Mrs Carter went early to bed. 'Don't stay up too late, dears,' said their mother. 'And remember to lock the annexe window.'

'I'll remember, Mum,' said Susan. 'See you in the morning.'

At ten o'clock, Paul folded his sleeping bag into a roll, took down the collar and lead, said goodbye to Susan and tip-toed up the side way. Fortunately he met no one on his short journey to the copse, and the moon riding high in the sky guided him to the picnic spot. In the shelter of a bush near the weeping willow, Paul struggled into his sleeping bag, and zipped up the side until only his face was showing. The quietness was broken by the almost sleepy swish of leaves, and the rustlings of small animals hiding amongst the undergrowth. Time passed, and Paul found himself overcome by drowsiness. In vain he tried to keep himself awake by doing simple sums in his head, and re-telling himself the last story he had read. But all to no avail. Paul fell asleep. He awoke to feel a rough tongue licking gently at his cheek. Paul opened his eyes and gazed into the golden-flecked eyes of Foxy. For a moment Paul did not dare to move, then as the fox's

eyes grew even brighter with pleasure of recognition, he unzipped his sleeping bag and sitting up, flung both arms round Foxy's neck.

'You haven't forgotten me after all,' Paul murmured, and with a gentle movement he slipped the collar over the cub's head. At first Foxy struggled violently, but as Paul fondled his ears and stroked his back, he calmed down, and allowed himself to be led back to Burley Avenue.

Susan took a long time to wake, but when at last she opened the kitchen door, she stared unbelievingly at Foxy, then jumped about in sheer joy.

'Shush!' whispered Paul. 'Not so much noise. You'll wake Mum and Dad.'

'I just can't believe it. Where did you find him?'

Paul told her the brief story, and as she listened, Susan's eyes widened. 'He actually found you.' She, too, flung her arms round the cub's neck. 'I always knew you were a clever old Foxy. I've filled a dish with food and another with milk just in case, but I still feel I'm dreaming.' Leading Foxy down the garden path to the shed, they watched him gulp down the food and empty the bowl of milk, then curl up in the box. It was as if he had never been away. 'Now do you believe it?' asked Paul.

'If he's still there tomorrow, I shall,' said Susan.

Susan and Paul kept the news of Foxy's return a secret from everyone except their parents and Gita. Gita shared their delight and brought down a bag containing chicken pieces. She eyed the cub thoughtfully.

'He doesn't look starved and you've groomed him beautifully.'

'He needed it,' answered Paul. 'His fur was matted with lumps of dried earth. He's been living rough, all right.'

'But loving every minute of it,' said Gita.

'How can you know?' Paul was puzzled.

'By the look in his eyes. Don't you see what I see? Foxy's homesick.'

Susan and Paul looked at her in shocked disbelief. 'But this is his home,' blurted out Susan at last.

Gita shook her head. 'Not any more. Foxy has tasted freedom, briefly, I know, but long enough to find a home for himself. Otherwise, why should he get earth on himself?'

Paul still refused to accept it. 'I don't believe you. You should have seen him scampering round and round the garden this morning. It was as if he were saying "thank you".'

'But how does he feel when he's put back in a closed and boarded up shed?' persisted their Indian friend. 'Oh, but don't take any notice of me. My mum always says I see something where there is nothing. Are you telling Brian?'

Paul shook his head. 'It isn't because I don't trust him, but it isn't fair to burden him with a secret he might not be able to keep.'

Gita nodded. 'I think that is wise. Now I must go back and make some more garlands for the fair. I have a beautiful one made for each of you to wear at the fête.'

'You won't catch me wearing a paper garland,' said Paul. 'I'd look proper daft as my Grandma would say.'

Gita's eyes twinkled. 'Then you might be the odd one out. Lots and lots of people have already promised to buy one. They want it to be the most colourful fête ever. Today we make more to festoon the stall. Let's hope the weather will be good.'

The weather was all they hoped for. The sun

shone in a cloudless blue sky and with the stalls set up, the roundabouts turning to blaring music, and more than a few wearing or carrying paper flower garlands, the Common had never looked so festive. The professional photographers clicked their cameras incessantly.

Gita and Susan entered for the sack race and tied at the finish. Paul and Brian entered for the fifty and hundred yards sprint, and in spite of Paul's lightness and speed, Brian with his powerful feet forged ahead and won both events. Paul took his defeat well, and even consented to wear a garland of poppies when he saw Gita slip another of marigolds over Brian's head. Then suddenly he grabbed Paul by the arm. 'Come on, it's the grown ups race now. I wouldn't miss it for anything.'

Paul and Susan's father got off to a good start, but in spite of being shorter and stouter, Mr Peters' training as a jogger stood him in good stead. Puffing and heaving, he lunged forward into first place at the finishing flag.

Brian's joy was unbounded. 'Now who says I'm boasting,' he crowed. 'Good old Dad. He can take anyone on.'

Paul did not answer, but stared down at Brian's running shoes. In his mind's eye he was seeing the Plaster of Paris cast his father had taken. Brian went to the changing tent where his father and Mr Peters were already putting on their ordinary shoes. Brian and Paul did likewise, but when Brian's attention was diverted, Paul switched Brian's left footed plimsoll for one of his own. In the excitement of winning and going up with his father to receive their prizes from the Mayor, Brian did not notice. Paul put his and Brian's shoe into his holdall, and joined Susan and his father at the refreshment stall. Mrs Carter poured them a fresh cup of tea, added an iced cake and charged them twenty pence. 'I reckon this will be a good day for the Old People's Home,' remarked his father. 'Should make them enough money to buy them the two colour television sets they so badly need. Sorry you and I were amongst the also rans, Paul.'

'Doesn't matter,' said Paul. 'Brian will be the loser in the long run.'

'And just what do you mean by that?' asked his father, drily. 'I thought you and Brian had buried the hatchet ages ago.'

'It can always be dug up again,' answered Paul.

'Aren't you enjoying yourself?' asked his mother, adding teasingly, 'I must say the garland of poppies suits you. Don't you agree, Susan?'

'I think Paul's got more than poppies on his mind.' Then in a whisper, she went on, 'I saw you make the switch when someone swung the tent opening wide.'

Paul took off the garland. 'Then you know.'

Susan nodded. 'Do we challenge him now?'

'Not without the evidence. And I don't want to miss the fireworks for Brian or for Foxy.'

As soon as dusk fell, the first Catherine Wheel burst into full flowering, and the first star shower rocket soared and burst high over their heads. Another and another followed until the whole sky seemed alight with all the colours of the rainbow. The set piece showing an elderly man and woman holding a banner bearing the words THE OLD WHITE HOUSE completed the show and brought the fête to a triumphant climax. The outburst of applause was reward enough for all the organisers. In little groups the people began to leave the Common. Mrs Carter stacked the last of her plastic tea mugs, bade goodbye to the last of her helpers, and clung to her husband's arm. 'It's been wonderful, but now I'm so tired, that I don't know how I shall walk home.'

'You don't have to,' replied her husband. '"Matty's" waiting for us in a side road.' Gita joined them for the ride, while her mother and father took what was left of the groceries back to the shop.

'Paul's so quiet, I think he's lost his tongue,' she said teasingly. 'Or perhaps it's my poppy garland he's holding. It makes him drowsy even though the flowers are only made of paper.'

'Paul is thinking of plimsolls or rather of a Plaster of Paris mould,' said Susan.

'A mystery,' exclaimed Gita. 'Why don't you tell us, Paul?'

'I will when we get home.'

'Matty' snorted to a standstill, and soon they were all in the sitting room. Paul took out the plaster cast from a shelf in the cupboard, and compared it with the one he had exchanged. 'You see,' he said, fitting the real shoe into the rough cast. 'It fits and it belongs to Brian, although it's not one he uses at school. There's no name inside. I expect it's one of a spare pair. I nicked it for one of mine in the changing tent.'

Mr Carter looked disturbed. 'Are you sure about it? How will he know the one he has belongs to you?'

'Paul's already explained,' said Susan. 'It will have Paul's name inside. All our school kit has to be marked.'

'Then what do we do?' asked Mrs Carter. 'Oh, dear, I do so hate rows.'

'This is one you'll have to put up with, Mum,' answered her son, his eyes glinting as the door bell rang. 'Ten to one, that's him now.'

Brian was not alone. Mr Peters stood beside him. 'Oh, hello, Paul. All right, we'll both come in, but only for a moment.' He looked at his son with pride. 'Me and Brian have done some useful running this afternoon.'

'And you might do some more tomorrow,' said Paul, leading the way into the sitting room. 'How would you like to be fined for trespassing and wilful damage, Brian?'

Brian looked at Paul as if he had taken leave of his senses. 'I don't know what you're

89

getting at! All I came for was to pick up the shoe you picked up by mistake.'

Paul pointed to the cast and the shoe. 'Anything strike you about them?'

'They match,' said Brian. 'How . . . how?'

'Don't play the innocent,' said Paul. 'That cast was made from a footprint left by the person who sawed through the slats and let Foxy loose that night. And that person was you.' Paul almost shouted the words. 'You rotten pig. You pretended you wanted to be friends with us, but all the time you were hatching your dirty little plot. Easy enough for you to recognise the rough edges as saw marks, and what a clever touch getting us to go down to the Police Station.'

Brian's face went white, and his eyes turned pleadingly towards his father. 'Tell . . . tell them, Dad,' he said hesitantly.

Mr Peter's normal florid complexion turned an even deeper shade of red. For a moment there was silence, then dragging the words out, he said, 'You're accusing the wrong person, kid. I'll not stand hearing my lad called names when the blame belongs to me.'

'*You* helped Foxy escape,' said Gita.

'Aye. Those shoes were my practice shoes I used years ago. They always brought me luck, so as Brian has big feet, I lent them to him today. Seems I brought him a packet of trouble instead. I'll pay for the damage, Mr Carter, if you'll drop charges, but I'll never apologise for what I did. Foxes are vermin and vermin they always will be in my estimation.'

'How could you be so cruel?' said Susan. 'We always meant Foxy to go free when he was old enough to fend for himself.'

Mr Peters ignored her and slapped two five pound notes on the table. 'That should cover any damage I've caused.'

'No it won't,' said Brian, closer to tears than anyone had ever seen him. 'You've just lost me three friends.'

'Rubbish,' said his father, no whit abashed by his confession. 'They've nothing against you. If they don't want to speak to me in the future, I can take it. So stop snivelling, lad. Pick up the shoe, and let's get going.'

Mr Carter got between Brian and his father. 'Not so fast, Mr Peters. I haven't yet said whether I'm going to sue or not. And another thing. What sort of a father are you who stays quiet while my son hurls one accusation after another at yours? Only when Brian began pleading did you come clean. If you aren't ashamed of yourself, you ought to be. And Brian isn't going with you. Right now he's staying to have supper with his friends while I think things over. What's more, you can take back your miserable ten pounds. Donate it to the Old White House, but don't try and bribe me with it.' Thrusting the notes into Mr Peters' unresisting hand, he almost pushed him towards the front door.

'Oh Mr Carter, I don't know what to say,' said Brian, as Paul's father returned.

'There's nothing *to* say.'

'You said plenty, Dad,' said Paul. 'I've never heard you slam into anyone like that before.'

'Mr Peters deserved it. I suppose I oughtn't to say it, seeing as how he's your father, Brian, but I think he's learned something tonight that he won't forget in a hurry.'

'Will you sue him?' asked Brian.

'Of course not, but it might make life a little bit easier for you, Brian, if he's left in doubt for a bit.'

Supper was a silent affair. All the children

were stunned by the sudden turn of events. Gita was so tired that she could hardly eat any of the good things Mrs Carter had provided, and Brian's thoughts were in a turmoil. He wished he never had to return to his own home, but when the time for parting came and Gita left with her parents, Mrs Carter made things easier for him. 'Cheer up, Brian,' she began. 'It's all right. Do you understand? Your father's got plenty to think about, and you can come over here whenever you like.' Brian thanked her and left.

Next morning when Paul and Susan went down to the shed, disorder again met them. As before the bedding was strewn all over the floor, the tools were scattered and an attempt had been made to gnaw through the solidly boarded up shed.

'Gita's right,' said Paul sorrowfully. 'We can't keep Foxy much longer. He wants and deserves to be free.'

For three days they made a special fuss of him, grooming him and feeding him every luxury they could lay their hands on, but always at the side of the dustbin.

'Why not in the garden?' asked Susan.

'Because I want to fix in his memory the spot where he can always be sure of finding food. It may not work, but on the other hand it might. It's worth a try anyway.'

At last the day came when Foxy was given his freedom. As dusk fell, they put him on his lead and set out. Gita met them at her front gate. 'No one told me, but I knew you would do the right thing.'

'Come with us, Gita,' said Susan.

Gita nodded. 'Why haven't you told Brian? Don't you trust him even now?'

'It isn't Brian, it's his father we don't trust. If he got wind of Foxy's whereabouts, he'd be after him again, if only to spite Dad.'

'Poor Brian. I'm sorry for him, but I'm glad now you're real friends,' said Gita falling into step beside them. 'Where are you taking Foxy?'

'We're letting him take us,' said Paul.

Foxy strained at the leash and Paul had all he could do to hold him in check. Foxy skirted the common and took the now so familiar path towards the Old White House. On the out-skirts of the copse he paused, sniffing the air as if to get his bearings, or assuring himself of safety, then he lurched across the rutted ground. Beyond a group of saplings was the huge, old and beautiful weeping willow, its fronded greenish-yellow branches falling like a canopy to the ground. Once inside they were in a world apart, a world of branches, gnarled, twisted roots and silence.

Paul slipped off the collar. 'To think we were so close to him that day and didn't know,' said Paul.

Foxy's eyes were bright with joy and recognition. With a pat from each of the children, he gave them one last backward glance, then wriggled out of sight down a hole among the roots, so carefully camouflaged with undergrowth that not even a glimpse of his pointed nose could be seen.

'Goodbye, Foxy,' said Susan softly. 'We didn't have to find you a new home after all. You found one for yourself. I wonder if we shall ever see or hear anything of you again? I don't suppose we shall.'

But Susan was wrong. Every night, Mrs Carter or the children hid a bowl of milk and some nourishing food behind the dustbin. Every morning both bowl and plate were empty. Paul's idea had proved good. Foxy had a good memory. Of course the nightly visitor could have been a cat, but no one in the Carter family was prepared to believe it. From this they all drew comfort. Foxy might now only look upon them as his larder, but while he did, a little bit of him still belonged to them.